STEAM COOKING

LOCI COMPANY

AuthorHouse™
1663 Liberty Drive, Suite 200
Bloomington, IN 47403
www.authorhouse.com
Phone: 1-800-839-8640

First published by AuthorHouse 03/25/2008

ISBN: 978-1-4343-2110-7 (sc)

Printed in the United States of America
Bloomington, Indiana

This book is printed on acid-free paper.

authorHOUSE®

Content

Introduction

Seafood   *23*

Meat & Poultry   *39*

Vegetable & Egg   *49*

Rice & Dumpling   *59*

Dessert   *79*

Introduction

In southern China, cities and towns near the sea where fresh seafood and other farm stock are abound, steamed food has been enjoyed by many generations. Various sauces, pastes and pantry items are added to a dish for variety. Steamed Fresh Shrimps, Spare Ribs With Plum Sauce, and Chicken In Lotus Leaf Wrap are delicious and easy to make. Steamed dishes created in northern China include steamed pork dumplings (soup-filled) and Shizi Tou Meatballs. These delicacies take some patience and labouring in the kitchen. Many of these steamed food can be found in Asian noodle shops or restaurants. Fortunately for the time-conscious and busy individuals who prefer to eat at home, most of these foods can be found in the frozen food section in most supermarkets. All one need do is to steam them up before serving.

Steam cooking, pan searing, stir-frying and deep-frying are the four most common techniques in Chinese cooking. Whether it is seafood or meat, its flavour and texture vary, depending on whether it is steamed, pan-seared, stir-fried or deep-fried. The selection of which technique to use is based upon whether it is the one to help bring out the best of the ingredients. A general rule in Chinese cooking is that steam cooking is the first choice for those very fresh ingredients.

Steam cooking is **healthy** because it uses steam instead of oil to cook. The ingredients must be fresh. Steam cooking is **simple** because it can be done either using a wok or while cooking rice While the choice of materials and the right amount of steamed time are crucial to make a tasty dish, you don't need to be an expert! Steam cooking is also **energy conserving** because most seafood or light meat dishes takes less than 10 minutes, compared with at least 30 minutes while using a conventional oven. Best of all, multiple servings can be cooked at the same time by stacking up the steamer baskets in one wok!

Fresh seafood and chicken are the best ingredients to use for steam cooking because it preserves moisture and gives meat a smooth and fine texture. Root vegetables are also good for steam cooking because consistent high heat and moist air can cook through the surface of the vegetable through to its core, while still conserving its taste. Many dim sum dishes are steam cooked. Pot rice is a classic example of a one-pot meal in Chinese cooking in which rice and meat dish are cooked and served in the same pot.

This book covers the basics of steam cooking, from how to flavour a dish, the appropriate water level and other general rules to determine cooking time. It talks about some finishing techniques that can enhance the flavour of a dish. There are illustrative examples of utensils, common sauces, herbs, seasoning, and pantry items that can be used with steam cooking. There are recipes for meat, fish, vegetables and dim sum dishes. They are easy to follow and illustrated with full-colour photography.

Technique

Fresh ingredients, proper flavouring, a correct burner setting and cooking time are the key elements for making a successful and tasty steamed dish. From preparation, cooking, to adding the finishing touch, a great dish can easily be created one step at a time.

Preparation

CLEANING

All great cooking starts with cleaning. Clean and pat dry ingredient before applying marinade.

		Rinse	Soak	Scrub	Notes
S e a f o o d	Fish, Softshell Seafood & Mussels	✓			-
	Live clam		✓		Soak in cold water for at least 3 hours. Let clams open up to release sand and dirt. Discard any that have not opened.
	Crab, Oyster			✓	Use a thick towel to protect your hands against scratching by the hard shells.
Meat & Poultry		✓			-
V e g e t a b l e	Leaf Vegetable	✓	✓		Pull leaves off from stem and soak them in cold water for at least 10 minutes. Rinse out any soil that may be trapped in stem area. Repeat soak and rinse cycle 2 to 3 times.
	Egg Plant, Melon, Chayote, Pumpkin	✓			Cut away stem. If needed, peel before rinsing.
	Root Vegetable, e.g., potato, yam	✓			Peel and rinse. If needed, let stand in cold water until it is time to cook, to reduce darkening after peeling.

MARINATING

Why marinate?

The purpose of applying marinade is three-fold - e.g., flavouring, creating aroma, and conserving the natural taste of the ingredients. Sauces, herbs and pastes are important ingredients that can add flavour to the meat or seafood. Sesame oil and cooking wine will create an enticing aroma to a dish. Oil and cornstarch act as a "seal", so that your food retains natural flavours and moisture.

	Aromatic Agents	Flavouring Agents	Agents to Conserve Naturalness of Ingredients
Marinade	Sesame oil, cooking wine, herbs	Sauces, pastes, sugar, salt, condiments, herbs	Oil, Cornstarch

How long does meat or seafood take to marinate?

Fresh seafood or thinly sliced meat require only a few minutes to marinate before steam cooking. For meat that is thicker than 1/2 inch, or has been kept frozen for a long time, you should marinate for at least 3 hours.

What to marinate?

Meat and poultry needs marinades more than seafood. Vegetable or rice requires little to no marinade at all. A general rule for applying marinade is that "less is more". Additional flavour will be obtained from different sources either during or after the cooking. The following describes common ingredients of marinade by the food type. The quantity of which depends on the recipe selected.

Seafood

Fresh Seawater Fish, Crab, or Lobster are quite tasty on their own by steam cooking and therefore no marinade is required.

Shrimp and Scallop - Sesame oil and white pepper

Clam, Oyster, Lake-Water or River Fish can be dressed with sauces and pastes to create various flavour for steam cooking.

Meat

Beef - Sesame oil, sugar, light soy sauce, dark soy sauce, oyster sauce, rose cooking wine or

Shaoxin cooking wine

Pork - Sesame oil, sugar, soy sauce, and cornstarch

Lamb - Sesame oil, sugar, soy sauce, ginger cooking wine and garlic paste

Poultry

Chicken - Sesame oil, sugar, soy sauce, ginger cooking wine, and rose cooking wine or Shaoxin cooking wine

Duck or Goose - Sesame oil, sugar, soy sauce, ginger cooking wine and garlic paste

Vegetable, Tofu, Bean and Mushroom

Leaf Vegetable, Root Vegetable, Bean and Tofu - None

Shitake Mushroom - Sugar and ginger cooking wine

Rice and Glutinous Rice

Jasmine Rice, Semi-milled, Coloured or Organic Rice - No marinade is necessary for Chinese style steam cooking.

Glutinous Rice - For salty dishes, use soy sauce, oyster sauce, Hoisin sauce and oil to marinate. For sweet dishes, use brown sugar and oil as your marinade.

Cooking

BURNER SETTING AND COOKING TIME

Select burner setting to be either High, Medium, or Medium Low, depending on the food to be steam cooked. Steam cooking continues even after the burner is turned off. Allowing time for the steam to continue to penetrate through beneath the surface and cook the inside of the ingredient is important for preserving the smooth surface of a dish.

	Burner Setting	Cooking Time	"Burner-Off Cooking"	Steamed Dish
Seafood	High	Short	No	Moist, firm and tender
Shredded Meat, Ribs, Poultry, Egg Curd	Begin with Medium then turn to Low until done	Medium	Yes	Smooth, tender and juicy
Root Vegetable or Fatty Meat Dish	Medium Low	Long	Yes	Soft and "melt in the mouth"
	Typically Cooking Time for 6 - 8 oz ingredient: Short 7 to 10 minutes Medium 11 to 25 minutes Long Over 25 minutes			

SPECIAL HANDLING

Egg Curd - For someone who is new to steam cooking, making egg curd may proove especially difficult. The surface of the egg curd should be smooth and not rough like the surface of the moon. The secret behind making a smooth egg curd dish is to beat the eggs with either chicken stock or pre-boiled water that has already been cooled down to room temperature. Avoid using water straight from the tap. Let the steamed egg curd continue to sit in the covered wok after the burner is turned off also reduces the chance of overcooking the surface of the egg curd.

Pot Rice - It is a one-pot meal that contains rice, meat and vegetable. There are two stages in making this dish. The first stage is to make the rice. Before the rice is fully cooked, add the meat or vegetable on top of the bed of rice. The hot steam of the cooking rice will cook these toppings. The natural juice and aroma that come from the ingredients will be infused into the rice.

Finishing

Hot oil glazing and proper pairing of dipping sauce with a dish are methods that can further improve the overall taste and aroma of a steamed dish.

HOT OIL GLAZING

Pouring hot oil over on top of the steamed food and then add soy sauce caramelizes the surface of the ingredients. This technique adds a savory and aromatic flavour to almost all steamed food dishes.

DIPPING SAUCE

A smart pairing of the food and dipping sauce wonderfully enhances the flavour of the food. A good example is the use of Chinese ZhenJiang Black Vinegar on the Soup-filled dumplings. By itself, the dumpling may be a bit underwhelming. However, with the addition of black vinegar, the taste of the meat juice and the entire dumpling becomes exquisite.

Safety

While steam enables fast cooking, use proper utensils and a lot of common sense to avoid potential hazards.

Proper Water Level - Water level in a wok should be just below or ***at most 1 inch below the dish at any time***. When water level is low, always top it up with boiling water before continuing to cook. If steam cooking is more than 10 minutes, check on the water level every 10 - 15 minutes. Never cook on a dry wok or leave the wok boiling unattended.

Safely Transferring Food To The Table - With one hand, use a proper tool (e.g., a plate-pick) to pick up the hot dish out of the wok. With the other hand, hold an inverted wok cover below the dish to safeguard against falling or tilting due to sudden imbalance of movement.

Prevent Oil Splashing - When applying hot oil glazing, use a wok cover to shield yourself against possible splashing of hot oil.

Utensils

Steamers and plate-picks are kitchen products that are specifically made for steam cooking. In fact, the four essentials for steam-cooking at home are a steamer, a wok with cover, a heat-proof dish and a plate-pick.

Steamer

STAINLESS STEEL STEAM RACK

A round rack which is used to hold a dish above water in a wok. It typically ranges from 5 to 8 inches in diameter and stands about 1 to 3 inches tall. The deeper the liquid may be in the wok, the taller a steam rack is required.

STEAMER BASKET

Bamboo Steamer with Cover

This icon for steam cooking is commonly seen during dim sum hours at Chinese restaurants. Rice buns or dumplings may be steamed directly inside a bamboo basket without the need of a plate. Remember to use a plate to protect the baskets when you are cooking saucy dishes like turnip steak or squid with curry sauce. A bamboo steamer functions like a steam rack except that it has a round wall to protect the ingredients from over steaming. By stacking up the bamboo steamers, multiple servings may be cooked in one wok. For dim sum or home cooking, there are 6 in., 8 in. or 10 in. diameter steamers. Commercial steamers can be 3 or 4 feet wide.

Stainless Steal Steamer

More durable and more expensive than bamboo steamers, stainless steel steamer are more commonly used commercially than for cooking at home.

Pot and Wok

WOK WITH COVER

A wok is ideal for steam cooking because not only does its domed shape able to accommodate a bulky dish, a covered wok also provides more space for water vapour to circulate inside the wok, thus enabling the food to be steam cooked more evenly. A wok should be big enough to hold enough water to last steam-cooking for at least 20 to 30 minutes, without the need to refill. Typically a flat-bottom wok ranges from 10 to 18 inches in diameter and 3 to 5 inches in height. Most people would find a 15 in. diameter and 3 in. tall flat bottom wok adequate for steaming as well as other general cooking tasks at home.

STAINLESS STEEL BOILER

It has a pot, a cover, and one or multiple steamer basket inserts. It is perfect for steaming food, especially those which require a long time of cooking; e.g., chunky meat pieces or root vegetables. Each pot is about 5 to 6 inches tall and can hold a lot of water for steaming. The basket inserts are equipped with handles which make transferring food to the table more easily.

DONABE

(Don - na - bi), Donabe means "ceramic pot" in Japanese. Sometimes it is also referred to as an earth pot or a modernized sand pot. A donabe may be used to make pot rice, stew, casseroles, and other dishes that require slow cooking. Typically a donabe ranges from 5 to 10 in. diameter and 3 to 4 in. height. Larger and taller size pots can be used to make soups or stocks. Never put a dry donabe over a hot burner or else it will crack. Other than that, a donabe is easy to use and can last a long time.

Accessories

Along with plate-picks and heat-proof dishes, oven mittens are useful to have around to pick up steaming dishes. Be sure to have coasters for setting your dishes down on your kitchen table. Don't forget to keep some parchment paper handy too

PLATE-PICK

It a tool that is used to pick up a hot dish out of the wok of boiling water after steam cooking. There are two styles of plate-picks: one is designed to work like a large clip, and the other has 3 long claws. Either one can be opened up to hold a dish. For large and heavy dishes, please remember to hold the bottom of the dish with an oven cloth with one hand, even though you are using a plate-pick on the other hand, when transporting the dish from the wok to the table.

PARCHMENT PAPER

For cakes or rice buns, a piece of parchment paper may be placed in the steamer basket before placing the food in the steamer. For dumplings, you can use a leaf of Chinese cabbage, or any leafy Chinese vegetable, in place of parchment paper on the steamer.

HEAT-PROOF DISH

Ceramic Dish

Generally, any Chinese-made, "everyday use" kind of dishes, e.g., the all white or those with blue and white pattern ceramic dishes, can be used for steam cooking. American-made Corningware, or Pyrex, as well as other similar brands that are known to be heat proof, can also be used in steam cooking. For steamed egg curd dishes that may otherwise be difficult to clean, don't forget to apply a thin layer of oil in the dish before adding the ingredients. The egg curd remnants come out quite easily with a light scrub.

Stainless Steel Dish

There are various shapes and styles. Stainless steel bowls may be used for making steamed rice with meat and vegetables.

Flavouring

Sauces and Pastes

Sauces and pastes that are used on steamed dishes are either salty, garlicky, sour or spicy. These jars or bottles of sauces and pastes are packed with flavour and can add interesting variations to seafood, meat or vegetable dishes.

SOY SAUCE

Made from soybean, this opaque, dark brown sauce is used on almost all Chinese dishes. Soy sauce has a salty, earthy taste. Depending on the length of the curing process, there are Light Soy Sauce and Dark Soy Sauce. Light Soy Sauce is thinner and saltier and it is also commonly used as a dipping sauce as well as a marinade. Dark Soy Sauce is darker, thicker and slightly sweeter. It is used most often in marinade to add colour or flavour.

OYSTER SAUCE

A good oyster sauce should be made from oyster. This sauce has a savory seafood taste and it is frequently applied on beef dishes and as a topping sauce for steamed or boiled vegetables.

SALTY PRAWN PASTE (A.K.A. SHRIMP PASTE, PRAWN PASTE)

It is made from fermented ground prawn, pepper, salt, garlic and bean oil. Because the flavour is so concentrated, it has a pungent smell. A little of this paste is adequate to flavour up a dish or even a whole pot of soup. It is often used on steamed squid or stir-fry vegetable dishes.

BLACK BEAN AND GARLIC PASTE

Made with black bean and garlic, it has a salty and sweet garlicky flavour. It is frequently used on steamed or stir-fried meat, seafood or vegetable dishes.

OLIVE AND MUSTARD GREEN PASTE

Made with black olive and mustard greens, this salty but slightly sweet paste is frequently used together with black bean and garlic paste on steamed fish and meat dishes.

Oil

Oil in Chinese food is fully cooked before consumed. While peanut oil or corn oil are used to cook, sesame oil is used to marinate.

SESAME OIL

Use sparingly, while a few drops of sesame oil enhance the aroma and taste of food, an overdose will make your food bitter. It is frequently used to marinate seafood, meat and even noodles.

PEANUT OIL

It is the top choice of vegetable cooking oils in Chinese cooking. Using peanut oil to cook improves the flavour and aroma of the food, although it is more expensive than corn oil.

CORN OIL

It is a more common substitute for peanut oil in Chinese cooking. It is also healthier than peanut oil due to its lower cholesterol content.

Herbs and Seasoning

GARLIC

Frequently used in Chinese cooking to provide aroma and taste. It is often used with green onion and ginger on seafood or meat dishes.

SPRING ONION (A.K.A. SCALLION)

Either paired with garlic or ginger, the flavour of the spring onion is best infused into a steamed dish by pouring hot oil over these ingredients.

GINGER

It is often used on chicken, lamb or seafood dishes to enhance flavour. Shredded ginger is commonly used with ZhenJiang Black Vinegar as dipping sauce for pan-fried or SiuLungBao dumplings.

LOTUS LEAF

The lotus plant is grown abundantly in fresh water pools and water gardens in China and Japan. An average lotus leaf is about 2 x 1-1/2 feet large. A whole leaf is often used to wrap up rice or sticky rice together with meat, egg, or vegetables. After steam cooking, the scent of the lotus leaf is infused into the food.

ZHENJIANG BLACK VINEGAR (A.K.A. CHENJIANG DARK VINEGAR)

It is made with black glutinous rice (or sweet rice). It is dark in colour and has a piquant and smoky flavour. It has a mature and cultivated taste, and it is less acidic than balsamic vinegar.

RED VINEGAR

Made with red yeast rice, it has a distinctive red colour. It is often used as a dipping sauce for dumplings, steamed crabs, shark's fin soup, fried noodles or noodle soups.

Wine

Unlike western wines that are made with grapes, the majority of Chinese wines are made with grain like rice or wheat. These wines have a relatively high alcohol content. Depending on the brewing method and the ingredients, there are yellow wines and clear wines.

RICE WINE (A.K.A. SIUJIU)

Rice wine has a water-clear colour. They are either distilled once (e.g., plain wine), double distilled or triple distilled. The more time a rice wine is distilled, the higher the alcoholic content. Korean rice wines are called Sojun and have less alcohol. Japanese rice wines are called sake. Rice wine can be used to cook fresh clams or mussels.

Cooking Wine

Cooking wines are salted to make them endure a long period of time after the bottle is opened. The standard salt content is 1.5%. Hence, they are not for drinking. Some cooking wines are flavoured like Rose Cooking

Wine and Ginger Cooking Wine.

RICE COOKING WINE

Salted rice wine which can be used with or without adding flavoured cooking wine. It is often used on chicken, beef or certain vegetable dishes.

SHAO HSIN RICE COOKING WINE

This wine is originated from a brewery in Shao Hsin. The recipe has a history of over 2000 years in China. The wine is brown and has a deep, fragrant and mellow taste. It is often used in marinating beef, chicken, or when stir-frying Chinese broccoli.

ROSE COOKING WINE

Made with wheat flour and rose, this water-clear wine enhances flavour of meat. It is often used with plain rice wine or ginger wine on chicken, lamb or beef dishes.

GINGER COOKING WINE

Rice-based cooking wine combined with ginger juice. It is often used in marinating chicken and lamb.

Pantry

Fuyu, salted fish and Chinese sausages are strong in flavour. They are either steamed with meat, fish, vegetables or rice. Shiitake mushrooms are commonly used in soup and steamed dishes for an earthy and woodsy aroma. Sundried scallop brings a subtle sea salt taste to a dish. These are but a few of the many pantry items in a Chinese kitchen.

FUYU (A.K.A. SALTY VEGETARIAN CHEESE, SALTY SOYBEAN CHEESE OR CHINESE CHEESE)

It is fermented dried tofu with the addition of rice wine or chili. Its existence was documented as early as 5 A.D. in China. The most common fuyu seen in Chinese supermarkets are either the creamy white fuyu or the red fuyu. White fuyu is frequently used on lamb or stir-fried vegetables. Red fuyu tastes sweeter. It is often used on roast chicken dishes. Fuyu is also an acquired taste. To choose a good jar of fuyu, gently turn the jar upside down. If you see flakes of fuyu that float up like a snow globe, then the fuyu is good.

SALTED FISH

Yellow croakers, thread fins or mackerels are dried and salted before being sold either whole or in portions. The jar of salted fish in oil can be kept in a fridge for up to a year. Salted fish may be used on pork, vegetable, or fried rice dishes.

CHINESE PORK SAUSAGE (A.K.A. LAP CHEONG, YUN CHEONG)

It is cured meat that is made with salted pork and bacon, it is air-dried and has a deep red color with "marbles" of bacon. Pork liver sausages have a darker brown colour.

DRIED SHIITAKE MUSHROOM

This is commonly used in many Cantonese steamed dishes. The top-grade dried Shiitake mushrooms are from Japan. Before cooking, these dried mushrooms need to be soaked in water at room temperature for at least 30 minutes, or until the mushrooms are soft to the touch of hand. It is customary to save the top part of the mushroom water for further culinary use on the same dish. For example, when you're making pot rice that uses shiitake mushroom, the mushroom water is added to the pot to cook rice.

SUN-DRIED SCALLOP (A.K.A. DRIED SCALLOP, YIU CHU, GAN BEI, YUEM BAI)

Sun dried scallop has a deep, mellow sea salt taste. It is a rather expensive ingredient that is often bought in dozens as a wedding present, according to Chinese customs. For best culinary results, dried scallops need to be soaked in water at room temperature for at least an hour, before marinating in ginger cooking wine, and then used in cooking.

DRIED SHRIMP

Dried shrimps are made by drying seawater shrimps under the sun. They give a fresh seafood taste to a dish and they are less expensive than fresh shrimps or sun dried scallops.

SALTED TURNIP (A.K.A. PRESERVED TURNIP, SALTED RADISH)

It can be found in the refrigerated section of a Chinese supermarket. It is often used with flank steak to make a steamed dish. (See page 40 for an example).

MUSTARD GREEN (A.K.A. PRESERVED VEGETABLE)

Preserved vegetables come in three different flavours, e.g., salty, pickled or chili hot. Chili hot mustard greens have red chili powder flakes on the mustard greens Chili hot mustard greens can be used on either beef or pork dishes. The salty mustard green is dry and has no liquid surrounding it in a package. It has a tinge of sweetness and is often used on pork or fish dishes. The sour mustard greens are pickled and sold inside a bag of vinegar and brine. Like the salty mustard green, sour mustard green are also used on pork or fish dishes.

SOUR PLUM (A.K.A. MEI ZI)

Sour and salty, it is often used on pork and fish dishes. An example is the Sour Plum Spare Ribs which is a classic Cantonese dish that is still seen in dim sum restaurants.

Rice and Vermicelli

SCENTED RICE

White jasmine rice from Thailand is often the defacto rice in many Chinese families. They are white and scented after steam cooking. When cooking scented rice, the rice to water ratio is 1 to 1-1/2. The rice rises to more than double its size after cooking.

SEMI-MILLED RICE

Red rice and brown rice are semi-milled. It is rich in vitamins B's and not as smooth-tasting as the fully milled rice. When cooking these semi-milled rice, it is best to add some oil to marinate. Add enough water to cover the rice when steam cooking. The rice only rises slightly after it is cooked.

GLUTINOUS RICE (A.K.A. STICKY RICE)

It uses less water but takes a longer time to cook than rice. Glutinous rice is more filling than milled or semi-milled rice. Soy sauce, oyster sauce, sugar and oil are often needed to flavour glutinous rice before steam-cooking. It is often used to make lotus leaf rice wraps. Purple glutinous rice is a popular ingredient for dessert in China and South East Asia.

BEAN THREAD VERMICELLI

Unlike most vermicelli that is made with rice, bean thread vermicelli is made with green beans and peas. It becomes transparent and bland-tasting when cooked. Bean thread vermicelli is best used in saucy and flavourful steamed dishes, to absorbs liquid as well as the flavour.

Frozen Food

Many delicious food that used to take a lot of labouring in the kitchen to make in the old days are now available in the frozen food section of many supermarkets. Simply steam them up and enjoy!

SIU LUNG BAO DUMPLINGS

Delicate and delicious, these pork dumplings have broth inside when they are cooked.

MINI STICKY RICE

This popular dim sum dish is made with sticky rice, chopped shiitake mushroom, sausage and shredded meat wrapped in a lotus leaf. The size of a large, traditional lotus leaf sticky rice wrap is reduced to snack size, to appeal to younger generations.

DIM SUM

Various kinds of rice buns, shrimp dumplings, and beef meatballs.

SEAFOOD

Steamed Lobster
With Rice Wine and Garlic Sauce

Steamed fresh lobster has a natural sweet taste. In this recipe, the flavours of the garlic and rice wine are pleasantly infused into the steamed lobster.

Prep Time   15 minutes
Cooking Time   10 minutes

Serves 1 to 2

1	lb	Lobster Tails

Sauce
2	cloves	Garlic, finely chopped. Divided into 2 parts.
3	tbsp	Rice Wine
2	tbsp	Corn Oil or Peanut Oil
1/8	tsp	Salt

1. Use a pair of kitchen scissors, cut lobster tails crosswise into 1 inch long pieces. Remove soft shells but leave the back shells on.
2. Put lobsters on a large heat-proof dish, back side down. Sprinkle half of the chopped garlic on top of the lobster pieces.
3. Make boiling water using a wok. When water is boiled, place lobster dish on a steam rack in center of wok. Water level should be just below the dish.
4. Cover wok and steam lobster for 10 minutes or until lobster pieces turned red.
5. In a skillet, heat oil and the remaining garlic over medium high heat. When garlic starts to release its aroma, add and stir rice wine and salt into oil. Stir.
6. When steamed lobster is ready, open wok cover and take out lobster dish.
7. Pour garlic and rice wine sauce on top of lobster and serve immediately.

Squid
With Salty Prawn Sauce

This easy-to make steamed dish uses salty prawn paste as the main flavouring ingredient. This dish is frequently seen in dim sum restaurants. It is also good with tea and steamed rice.

Prep Time   10 minutes
Cooking Time   15 minutes

Serves 1

1		Squid, cleaned and cut into pieces

Marinade and Sauce

1	tsp	Garlic, finely chopped
½	tsp	Ginger, grated or finely chopped
1/8	tsp	Sesame Oil
1/8	tsp	White Pepper
1	tbsp	HsaoHsin Cooking Wine
½	tbsp	Salty Prawn Paste (a..k.a. Prawn Paste, Shrimp Paste)
½	tsp	Corn Oil or Peanut Oil

1. Make boiling water in a sauce pan, use a large skewer to blanch the squid in the boiling water for 2 minutes. Remove squid from water, turn on tap and run cold water on squid pieces for 1 minute. Use a paper towel to wipe squid pieces off excess water.
2. Place squid pieces in a mixing bowl, add marinade. Use a pair of bamboo chopsticks (or a spoon) to blend ingredients together.
3. Make boiling water using a wok. When water is boiled, place the dish of marinated squid on a steam rack in center of wok. Cover wok and steam for 15 minutes.
4. Serve hot.

Variation: Substitute salty prawn paste with ½ tea spoon of curry powder to make curry flavour steamed squid

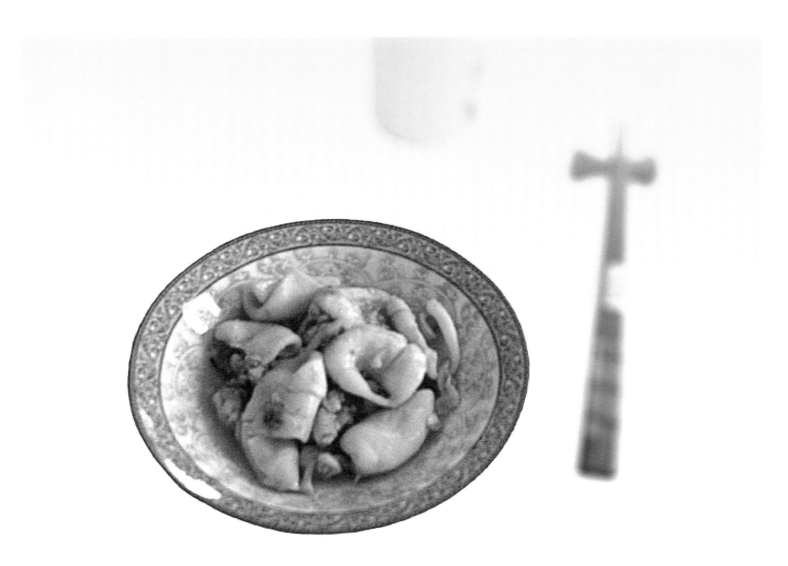

Tiger Shrimp Tofu
With Oil and Soy Sauce

Some people say tofu is like a blank canvas that goes well with anything. This simple but tasty dish uses fresh tiger shrimp, oil and soy sauce to bring out fresh bean taste of the tofu.

Prep Time   10 minutes
Cooking Time   8 minutes

Serves 1 - 2

1	lb.	Tofu (a.k.a. Bean Curd, Romaji), sliced
6		Fresh Tiger Shrimps, shelled and de-veined
2	tbsp	Spring Onion, chopped. Divided into 2 parts

Marinade
1/8 tsp   Sesame Oil
1/8 tsp   White Pepper

Sauce
3 tbsp   Corn Oil or Peanut Oil
1-½ tbsp   Soy Sauce

1. Turn stove on medium high and begin to make a pot of boiling water using a steam boiler. Water should start boiling in 7 to 10 minutes.
2. Put tofu on a heat-proof dish, set aside.
3. Put tiger shrimps in a small mixing bowl, marinade with sesame oil and white pepper.
4. Place tiger shrimps and one-half of the chopped spring onions on tofu.
5. When water is boiled, put dish in steamer. Cover boiler and steam tofu and tiger shrimps over medium high heat for 8 minutes.
6. Open boiler cover and place remaining chopped spring onion on top of shrimps and tofu.
7. At about 1-½ minutes before the tiger shrimps and tofu finish steaming, pour corn oil into a small saucepan and cook over Medium High heat for about 1 minute or until oil is sizzling hot. Turn off heat.
8. Add the remaining chopped onion on top of the shrimps and tofu.
9. Pour hot oil and then soy sauce over the spring onion, tiger shrimps and tofu.
10. Serve hot with steamed rice.

Salmon Fillet
With Ginger and Spring Onion

Keep an eye on the time when steaming this dish. Salmon fillets are most tender and delicious when they are slightly undercooked. The hot oil caramelizes the salmon and brings an aromatic flavour to the dish.

Prep Time	*5 minutes*
Cooking Time	*7 minutes*

Serves 1 - 2

8	*oz.*	*Salmon Fillet (skin-on, boneless)*
2	*slices*	*Ginger, shredded*
1		*Spring Onion, shredded. Divided into 2 parts.*
Sauce		
3	*tbsp*	*Corn oil or Peanut Oil*
1-½	*tbsp*	*Soy Sauce*

1. Turn stove on medium high and begin making a wok of boiling water. Water should start boiling in about 7 to 10 minutes.
2. Place salmon fillet on a heat-proof dish, skin side down.
3. Add the shredded ginger and one-third of the spring onion on top of the salmon fillet.
4. When water is boiled, cover wok and steam the salmon fillet over medium high heat for 7 minutes.
5. At about 1 ½ minutes before the salmon finishes steaming, pour corn oil or peanut oil into a small saucepan and cook over medium high heat for about 1 minute or until oil is sizzling hot. Turn off stove.
6. At the 7 minute mark, turn off stove and open wok cover. Drain off any excess liquid. Then add the remaining spring onion on top of the salmon fillet.
7. Pour the hot oil and then soy sauce over the ginger, spring onion and salmon fillet.
8. Serve hot with steamed rice.

Oyster In The Half-Shell
With Black Bean Sauce and Vermicelli

Pacific oysters are plump and juicy. They can be steamed, deep fried or used as an ingredient to make rice soup. The bean thread vermicelli that sides with the saucy oysters wonderfully absorbs the flavour of the black bean sauce.

Prep Time	20 minutes
Cooking Time	10 minutes

Makes 3

3		Fresh Pacific Oysters
1	oz	Bean Thread Vermicelli, soaked in a bowl of cold water. Set aside.

Marinade and Sauce

½	tbsp	Garlic, minced
2	tbsp	Black Bean Paste
1		Red Chili, finely chopped
2	tbsp	Corn Oil

1. Clean oysters. Wear an oven mitten or use a thick towel to hold down and pry open oysters with a oyster knife. The meat of the oyster stays on one side of the shell. Discard the other side of the shell that is empty. Place half-shells of oysters on a heat-proof dish.
2. Put garlic, black soybean paste and red chili in a small mixing bowl. Mix ingredients with a spoon. Divide marinade into 3 parts. Spoon marinades onto each of the three oysters.
3. Divide bean thread vermicelli among the oysters. Place bean thread vermicelli on top or at side of oyster,
4. Steam over High for 10 minutes.
5. Caramelize with hot oil.
6. Serve hot.

Steamed Crab Dung Guan
With Black Bean and Minced Pork

Dung Guan is a small town in southern China, near the provincial capital city of Guang Zhou. This recipe combines the ground pork, crab, black bean and egg to make a tasty and hearty dish.

Prep Time	10 minutes
Cooking Time	15 minutes

Serves 3 - 4

1		Live crab, cleaned
3		Large Eggs
1	cup	Water
2	tsp	Corn Oil
½	tsp	Salt
4	oz	Ground Pork

Marinade		
2	tbsp	Light Soy Sauce
1	tsp	Cornstarch
½	tsp	Sesame Oil
2	tsp	Black Bean Paste

Glazing		
1	tbsp	Corn Oil

1. Marinate ground pork in a mixing bowl. Pour mixture in a shallow heat-proof dish. With a pair of bamboo chopsticks (or a fork), beat egg, corn oil, salt and water together for 3 to 4 minutes. Pour egg mixture into the dish that contains the ground pork. Put the cleaned crab on top.
2. Make boiling water using a wok. When water is boiled, place the crab and ground pork dish on a steam rack in centre of wok and steam cook for 15 minutes.
3. Heat up the 1 tbsp corn oil in the microwave oven. When the crab and ground pork dish is ready, pour the hot oil on top of the crab.
4. Serve hot with steamed rice.

Steamed Clams
With Ginger and Rice Wine Sauce

Small clams are used in this recipe because they are more tender than larger ones. The rose cooking wine adds aroma and the water-clear rice wine brings out the fresh taste of the clams.

Prep Time	5 minutes
Material Stand Time	2 hours
Cooking Time	15 minutes

Serves 1 - 2

1	lb	Fresh Small Clams.
1		Spring Onion, shredded
2	slices	Ginger, shredded

Rice Wine Sauce

1/3	cup	Rice Wine
1	tsp	Rose Cooking Wine
1	tsp	Corn Oil

1. Soak clams in cold water for 2 hours to let out sand
2. Put clams in a shallow heat-proof dish. Blend spring onion, ginger and rice wine sauce into the dish.
3. Make boiling water using a wok. When water is boiled, place dish on a steam rack in center of wok.
4. Cover wok and steam for 12- 15 minutes under medium high heat.
5. Open wok cover and discard any clam that is unopened.
6. Serve hot.

Meat & Poultry

Turnip Steak
With Green Onion

This simple dish is tasty when paired with steamed rice. Traditionally, this recipe calls for hand-ground beef in order to create a smoother taste after steaming. However, store-bought ground beef is fine if you're in a hurry.

Prep Time   10 minutes
Cooking Time   8 minutes

Serves 1

6	oz	Flank Steak, finely chopped
2	tbsp	Salty Turnip (a.k.a. Salty Radish), coarsely chopped

Marinade
1	tbsp	ShaoHsin Cooking Wine
1/4	tsp	Sesame Oil
½	tsp	Light Soy Sauce
1/8	tsp	Sugar
1	tsp	Cornstarch (optional)

1. Rinse salty turnip with cold water. Drain and pad dry. Set aside.
2. In a small mixing bowl, use a pair of bamboo chopsticks (or a spoon) to mix marinade and beef together. Blend in salty turnip. Pour ingredients onto a heat-proof dish.
3. Make boiling water using a wok. When water is boiled, place dish in center of wok.
4. Cover wok and steam for 8 minutes over Medium High heat
5. Serve hot.

Variations:
Substitute salty turnip with either salty mustard greens or chili mustard greens.

Boneless Pork Chop
With Sour Plum and Chili

This recipe is a a variation of the classic dish of Sour Plum Spareribs using boneless pork chops instead of spareribs.

Prep Time   10 minutes
Cooking Time   10 minutes

Serves 1

5 oz	Boneless Pork Chop (cut into 1-in. dices)
1 tbsp	Garlic, chopped
2	Sour Plums, chopped
2	Sour Plums (as garnish, optional)
1	Small red chilli pepper, chopped
1	Small red chilli pepper (garnish, optional)

Marinade
½ tsp	Sesame oil
1 tbsp	Light Soy sauce
½ tsp	Sugar
1 tbsp	HsaoHsin cooking wine

1. In a large mixing bowl, mix pork and marinade together with a pair of bamboo chopsticks or a spoon. Blend in sour plum.
2. Place ingredients onto a heat-proof dish.
3. Cover wok and steam for 10 minutes.
4. (Optional) Garnish with sour plums and red chili pepper.
5. Serve hot.

Shizi Tou Meatballs
With Crab Meat and Crab Liver

Shizi Tou (Lion's Head) Meatballs is a well-known dish from Shanghai. The crab and the finely chopped pork bathed in chicken stock makes a delicious meal.

Prep Time   30 minutes
Cooking Time   25 minutes

Makes 4

½	lb	Pork Belly finely chopped
1		Live Crab, cleaned and have the "dead man's fingers" removed
1	cup	Chicken Stock
½	tsp	Salt
5	leaves	Nappa Cabbage

Marinade
2		Egg White
½	cup	Cornstarch
2	txp	Salt
3	tsp	Cornstarch
1	tsp	Ginger Juice
1/8	tsp	White Pepper
1	tbsp	Water

1. Steam cook the crab. Take out the meat and the liver in separate bowls. Set aside.
2. Put pork in a large mixing bowl, mix egg white, crab meat, and marinade together with a spoon.
3. Wear a pair of disposable latex gloves (or use clean bare hands), scoop out the pork mixture by hand from the mixing bowl, knead and then throw it at the side of the bowl. Repeat this action 30 - 40 times or until the pork mixture becomes sticky.
4. Form four 1½ - 2 in. balls using the pork mixture. Pinch a hole on top of each meat ball with a finger. Divide the crab liver into 4 parts. Fill each of the four meatballs with one part of the crab liver.
5. Put meat balls in a large heat-proof bowl. Put the nappa cabbage and ½ tsp. salt at a side of the bowl. Add chicken stock to cover about 80% of the meat balls.
6. Make boiling water using a wok. When water is boiled, place meatball dish on a steamer rack in center of wok.
7. Cover wok and steam for 25 minutes under medium high heat and then serve.

45

Lotus Leaf Chicken
With Shiitake Mushroom and Sausage

This is a popular Cantonese dish. The earthy scent of the lotus leaf is subtly infused into the chicken. Additionally, the fat and the saltiness of the sausage and the woodsy taste of the Shiitake mushroom accent the taste of the chicken.

Prep Time   10 minutes
Cooking Time   20 minutes

Serves 2

2		Boneless Chicken Thighs (cut into ½ in. pieces)
3		Dried Shiitake Mushroom, soak in cold water for 2 hours, Pat dry and cut into strips.
1		Chinese Sausage, soak in boiling water for 3 minutes. Pat dry and cut into pieces.
1		Lotus Leaf, soak and rinse in hot water for 5 minutes. Drain and set aside.

Marinade for Chicken

1	tbsp	Light Soy Sauce
½	tsp	Sugar
1	tbsp	HsaoHsin Cooking Wine
½	tbsp	Ginger Cooking Wine
1/4	tsp	Sesame Oil
2	cloves	Garlic, minced
3	pieces	Ginger, shredded

Marinade for Shiitake Mushroom

1/4	tsp	Sesame Oil
½	tsp	Sugar
1	tbsp	HsaoHsin Cooking Wine

1. In a large mixing bowl, blend in chicken with marinade with a pair of chopsticks. Set aside.
2. Marinade shiitake mushroom with sesame oil, HsaoHsin cooking wine, and sugar. Set aside for 15 minutes.
3. Wrap up chicken, Shiitake mushroom, and ginger in lotus leaf. Place wrap in a large bamboo steamer
4. Make boiling water using a wok. When water is boiled, place bamboo steamer in center of wok.
5. Cover wok and steam for 20 minutes under Medium High. Turn off stove and let stand for 10 minutes.
6. Open lotus leaf wrap and serve.

VEGETABLE & EGG

Lotus Root
With Sun Dried Scallop and Sausage

The lotus root will become tender and crunchy after it is steamed. Salty sun dried scallop and Chinese pork sausage wonderfully help to flavour the lotus root.

Prep Time   *10 minutes*
Cooking Time   *15 minutes*

Serves 2

2		Large Sun Dried Scallop
1		Chinese Pork Sausage
1		Lotus Root, peeled and shredded
1	tbsp	Spring Onion, shredded

Marinade
1	tsp	Ginger Cooking Wine
1/4	tsp	White Pepper
1	tsp	Cornstarch

1. Soak sun dried scallop in cold water for an hour. Drain and put into a small heat-proof dish. Add ginger cooking wine and steam over Medium High heat for 15 minutes. Shred and set aside.
2. Fill a wok with 2 inches of water. Turn stove on high and bring to a boil. Put in sausage and cook for 2 minutes. Drain and cut sausage at an angle into several 1/4 inch pieces.
3. In a mixing bowl, mix all ingredients and the remaining marinade together. Pour ingredients into a heat proof dish.
4. Make boiling water using a wok. When water is boiled, place dish on a steam rack in center of wok.
5. Cover wok and steam for 15 minutes over Medium High heat. Garnish with spring onion and serve immediately.

Fuzzy Squash
With Shrimp and Sun Dried Scallop

Fuzzy squash looks like a zucchini with short, little fuzzy white hairs. It is a vegetable harvested in summer. It has a fresh garden taste and slightly sweet when cooked.

Prep Time   10 minutes
Cooking Time   15 minutes

Serves 2

1		Large Sun Dried Scallop, soak in water for 1 hour, add ginger cooking wine and steam cooked for 15 minutes and then shredded into pieces.
4		Tiger Shrimps, shelled, deveined and coarsely chopped.
1		Fuzzy Squash, peel and cut into 1 inch rings
½	cup	Chicken Stock
½	tsp	Salt
1/4	tsp	Sugar

Marinade for Sun Dried Scallop
1   tbsp   Ginger Cooking Wine

Marinade for Tiger Shrimp
1/4   tsp   White Pepper
½   tsp   Sesame Oil

1. Marinade tiger shrimps.
2. Place fuzzy squash rings on a shallow heat-proof dish. Sprinkle salt and sugar on top.
3. Spoon shrimps on top of each ring of the fuzzy squash
4. Add chicken stock to dish.
5. Make boiling water using a wok. When water is boiled, place dish on a steam rack in center of wok.
6. Cover wok and steam for 15 minutes over medium high heat or until fuzzy squash is softened and can be pierced through with one chopstick.
7. Save the liquid as a soup and pour it into a bowl.
8. Serve fuzzy squash.

Steamed Three Vegetables
Eggplant, Sweet Potato and Yam

Sweet potatoes and yams are fibre-rich and are believed to have beautifying benefits. They are naturally sweet when cooked. Eggplant is believed to have multiple medicinal benefits such as reducing cholesterol and repairing blood vessels.

Prep Time   5 minutes
Cooking Time   15 - 20 minutes

Serves 3

1		Sweet Potato, cubed
1		Yam, cubed
1		Chinese Eggplant, cut into small (about 1/4 x 1 in.) pieces
½	tsp	Sugar

Marinade for Egg plant
1/8	tsp	Sea Salt
1	tbsp	Olive Oil or Corn Oil

1. Use a pair of chopsticks to blend egg plant and marinade together. Pour mixture in a heat-proof dish.
2. Put sweet potato in another heat-proof dish. Mix sugar with sweet potato.
3. Put yam in a third heat-proof dish.
4. Make boiling water using a 3-tier steamer boiler. When water is boiled, place each of the sweet potato, yam and egg plant dish into a different steamer basket and stack up on top of one another. Cover the top steamer basket and steam vegetables on medium high heat for 10 minutes.
5. Check water level at 10 minutes. Change the stacking order of the steamer baskets and continue to steam cook vegetables for another 5 minutes. Remove the steamer basket that contains the egg plants. Continue to steam cook the yam and the sweet potato for another 5 minutes or until vegetables are soft and can easily be pierced through with a chopstick.
6. Serve hot.

Steamed Egg Curd
With Spring Onion

It is amazing how the use of pre-boiled water changes the look of the steamed egg curd from one that resembles the surface of the moon into a fine and smooth finish. This dish is popular in Southern part of China. In Japan, steamed egg curd is often made in a cup, with addition of chicken, mushroom and other vegetables.

Prep Time   *10 minutes*
Cooking Time   *8 minutes*

Serves 2

1. In a mixing bowl, beat eggs and pre-boiled water or chicken stock together. Add salt and corn oil, beat again.

3		Large Eggs	1	tsp	Corn Oil
3/4	cup	Chicken Stock or Pre-boiled Water that is cooled down to room temperature	½	tsp	Rice Vinegar
			Sauce		
½	tsp	Green Onion, finely chopped	1	tbsp	Corn Oil
½	tsp	Salt	½	tbsp	Light Soy Sauce

2. Put a steam rack in centre of wok. Fill water up to 1/4 inch above the rack. Place a heat-proof dish on rack. Cover wok and turn stove on high.
3. When water in wok is boiled, pour egg mixture into the dish. Add rice vinegar and stir for two rounds. Cover wok and steam for 8 minutes under medium. Turn off stove and let stand for 10 minutes.
4. Add spring onion on top as garnish.
5. Heat up the 1 tbsp oil in a microwave oven. Then pour the hot oil and then the soy sauce to the steamed egg curd. Serve hot.

Variation:
Marinade 3 oz. minced pork with the following ingredients and then add to the egg mixture after step 1.

Marinade for pork		
1/4	tsp	Sugar
1	tbsp	HsaoHsin Cooking Wine
1/8	tsp	Sesame Oil
1	tbsp	Light Soy Sauce

56

RICE & DUMPLING

Steamed Rice
Scented Rice, Organic Brown Rice and Red Rice

Scented jasmine rice from Thailand has a fragrant aroma and just a tinge of sweetness. It is best eaten with saucy dishes. Semi-milled rice is rich in fibre and vitamin B, although it does not taste as good as the scented rice.

Prep Time   5 minutes
Cooking Time   15 minutes

Makes 3

Scented Rice
½   cup   Scented Jasmine Rice, rinsed and drained
3/4 cup   Water

Organic Brown Rice
½   cup   Organic Brown Rice, rinsed and drained
1/3 cup   Water
½   tsp   Corn Oil

Red Rice
½   cup   Red Rice, rinsed and drained
1/4 cup   Water
½   tsp   Corn Oil
1/8 tsp   Sugar (Optional)

1. Put scented rice, organic brown rice and red rice into heat-proof cups. Then add water. If marinade is needed, stir into water and rice mixture with a spoon. Put rice cups in a bamboo steamer.
2. Make boiling water using a wok. When water is boiled, place steamer in the center of wok. Water should cover about 1/3 of the cup.
3. Cover wok and steam for 15 minutes under medium high heat. Turn off stove and with wok covered, let rice cups stand for 10 minutes.
4. Serve hot.

Sticky Rice
With Pork Sausage and Shiitake Mushroom

Unlike plain-cooked scented rice, sticky rice is generously flavoured with various sauces, oil, seafood and meat. On a cold day, it makes a hearty meal guaranteed to warm you up.

Prep Time   20 minutes
Cooking Time   25 minutes

Makes 1

1	cup	Glutinous Rice (a.k.a. Sticky Rice)		**Marinade for Mushroom**		
			1/4	tsp	Sesame Oil	
½	cup	Water and Mushroom Water (See Step 45below)	½	tsp	Sugar	
			1	tbsp	HsaoHsin Cooking Wine	
1		Pork Sausage				
1		Sun Dried Scallop		**Marinade for Glutinous Rice**		
1	tbsp	Dried Shrimps	¼	tsp	Salt	
1		Dried Shiitake Mushroom	½	tsp	Sugar	
1		Shallot	1½	tbsp	Peanut Oil or Corn Oil	
1	tbsp	Peanut Oil or Corn Oil	½	tsp	Light Soy Sauce	
			½	tsp	Dark Soy Sauce	
Marinade for Sun Dried Scallop			½	tsp	Oyster Sauce	
1/4	tsp	Ginger Cooking Wine				

1. Soak sun dried scallop, dried shiitake mushroom, and dried shrimps in different mixing bowls for an hour.
2. Wash glutinous rice. Cook in boiling water for 2 minutes. Rinse with cold water. Drain and add marinade.
3. Fill a wok with 2 inches of water. Turn stove on and bring to a boil. Put sausage in hot water for 2 minutes. Drain and cut sausage into small pieces.
4. Drain sun dried scallop, add ginger cooking wine and steam for 10 minutes. Shredded and set aside.
5. Take shiitake mushroom from bowl. Remove stem. Squeeze off excess water. Pad dry with paper towel. Dice and add marinade. Skim and save the top part of the mushroom water and use it to cook glutinous rice.
6. Drain and shred dried shrimps.
7. Heat 1 tbsp of oil and saute shallot. Stir-fry sausage, sun dried scallop, dried shrimps and shiitake mushroom for 2 minutes. Add glutinous rice and stir fry for another minute.
8. Pour ingredients into a heat-proof bowl and steam over high heat for 20 minutes.
9. Serve hot.

Sticky Rice Wrap
With Chicken and Roast Pork

The summery lotus leaf scent is infused into the sticky rice. It is a popular dim sum dish in southern part of China.

Prep Time   *20 minutes*
Cooking Time   *10 minutes*

Makes 1

1	cup	Glutinous Rice (a.k.a. Sticky Rice)
1	pc	Dried Lotus Leaves, soaked in hot water for 15 minutes. Pat dry. Set aside.

Filling

½		Boneless Chicken Thigh
1	oz	Roast Pork
1		Chicken Gizzard
1		Chicken Liver
2		Shrimp, shelled and de-vein
1		Dried Shiitake Mushroom
1		Shallot
1	tbsp	Peanut Oil or Corn Oil

Marinade for Filling

¼	tsp	Salt
1	tbsp	Cornstarch

Marinade for Mushroom

1/4	tsp	Sesame Oil
½	tsp	Sugar
1	tbsp	HsaoHsin Cooking Wine

Marinade for Glutinous Rice

¼	tsp	Salt
½	tsp	Sugar
1-½	tbsp	Peanut Oil or Corn Oil
½	tsp	Dark Soy Sauce

1. Wash glutinous rice. Cook in boiling water for 2 minutes. Rinse with cold water. Drain and add marinade.
2. Steam glutinous rice for 20 minutes. Divide into 2 equal portions.
3. Soak dried shiitake mushroom in water for 30 minutes or until soften. Remove stems. Squeeze off excess water. Pat dry with paper towel. Dice and add marinade.
4. Chop shallot. Dice roast pork.
5. Clean and dice chicken, pork, chicken gizzard and chicken liver. Add marinade for filling.
6. Heat 1 tbsp of oil and saute shallot. Add ingredients for filling and stir-fry until cooked. Stir in the sauce. Dish up.
7. Grease Lotus Leaf. Put one portion of glutinous rice in the centre of the leaf and the one portion of the filling on top. Then put in the remaining portion of glutinous rice. Shape and wrap up.
8. Steam over High heat for 10 minutes and serve.

Chicken Pot Rice
With Shiitake Mushroom and Two Sausages

The chicken is flavoured by the salty sausages. The shiitake mushrooms bring a woodsy taste to the pot rice.

Prep Time   20 minutes
Cooking Time   25 minutes plus 10 minutes stand time

Serves 2

1. Fill a wok with 2 inches of water. Turn stove on and bring to a boil. Put sausage in hot water for 2 minutes. Drain and cut sausage into several 1/4 inch

1		Boneless Chicken Thigh, skin on.
1		Pork Sausage
1		Pork Liver Sausage
2	cups	Jasmine Rice
3	cups	Water and Shiitake Mushroom Water (See Step 2)
2		Dried Shiitake Mushrooms, soaked in cold water for ½ hour or until softened
1	tbsp	Chopped Spring Onion

Marinade for Shiitake Mushrooms

1/8	tsp	Sesame Oil
½	tsp	Sugar
1	tbsp	HsaoHsin Cooking Wine

Marinade for Chicken

1	tbsp	Light Soy Sauce
½	tsp	Sugar
1	tbsp	HsaoHsin Cooking Wine
½	tbsp	Ginger Cooking Wine
1/4	tsp	Sesame Oil
1	clove	Garlic, minced

Sauce

2	tbsp	Light Soy Sauce
½	tsp	Sugar
2	tbsp	Corn Oil

     pieces.

2. Squeeze off excess water from Shiitake mushrooms. Skim and save the top part of the mushroom water and use it to cook rice. Cut mushrooms into 1/4 in. strips. Marinate Shiitake mushrooms in a mixing bowl. Set aside.
3. Cut three 2 inches long slits across the chicken thigh. Marinate chicken.
4. Put rice, water and mushroom water in a ceramic pot (donabe). Turn stove on medium high. Bring rice and liquid to a boil. Cook for 10 minutes or until rice has absorbed almost all of the liquid in the pot and has formed a soft bed in the donabe. The rice is now ready for the chicken and other ingredients.
5. Lower heat to medium low. Add chicken, sausages, and mushrooms to the pot. Cover donabe and steam for 10 minutes. Garnish with spring onion. Cover donabe and let stand for 10 minutes before serving.
6. Heat oil and then add soy sauce together to make a dipping sauce for the pot rice.

Pork Pot Rice
With Olive and Salty Mustard Green

This salty and garlicky flavoured pork pot rice is very appetizing and easy to make.

Prep Time	*10 minutes*
Cooking Time	*25 minutes plus 10 minutes stand time*

Serves 2

12	oz	Ground Pork
1	clove	Garlic, minced
2	tbsp	Olive and Salty Mustard Green Paste
1	tbsp	Black Bean Paste
2	cups	Jasmine Rice
3	cups	Water

Marinade for Pork

1	tbsp	Light Soy Sauce
½	tsp	Sugar
½	tbsp	Rice Cooking Wine
1/4	tsp	Sesame Oil
1	clove	Garlic, minced

Sauce

2	tbsp	Light Soy Sauce
½	tsp	Sugar
2	tbsp	Corn Oil

1. Marinate ground pork in a mixing bowl. Spoon in olive and salty mustard green paste and black bean paste. Blend ingredients together.
2. Put rice and water in a ceramic pot (donabe). Turn stove on medium high. Bring rice and water to a boil. Cook for 10 minutes or until rice has absorbed almost all of the liquid in the pot and has formed a soft bed in the donabe. The rice is now ready for the pork.
3. Lower heat to medium low. Add pork to the pot. Cover donabe and steam for 10 minutes. Garnish with spring onion. Cover donabe and let stand for 10 minutes before serving.
4. Heat oil and then add soy sauce together to make a dipping sauce for the pot rice.

Siu Lung Bao
Soup-filled Pork Dumplings in a basket

Siu (Small) Lung (Basket) Bao (Bun, Dumpling) is a popular dim sum dish in Northern China. Don't forget to dip your dumplings with shredded ginger and ZhenJiang Black Vinegar.

Prep Time	20 minutes
Cooking Time	6 minutes

Makes 8

Wrapping

8		Dumpling Wraps

Filling

1	tbsp	Gelatine
3/4	cup	Water and Shiitake Mushroom Water (See Step 1)
4	oz	Ground Pork
2		Dried Shiitake Mushrooms, soaked in cold water for ½ hour or until softened
2	tbsp	Peanut Oil or Corn Oil
1	clove	Garlic, minced

Lining for Steamer Basket

1	leaf	Nappa Cabbage

Marinade for Pork

1½	tsp	Light Soy Sauce
1	tsp	Sugar
1/8	tsp	Pepper
1/4	tsp	Sesame Oil
1	tsp	Corn Oil

Dipping Sauce

2	tbsp	ZhengJiang Black Vinegar
1	tsp	Ginger, shredded

1. Squeeze excess water off of Shiitake mushrooms. Skim and save the top part of the mushroom water and use it in the next step. Dice mushrooms and marinate them in a mixing bowl. Set aside.
2. In a saucepan, dissolve gelatine powder into water. Heat and stir until gelatine is completely dissolved. Remove from heat. Cool and then cut into cubes.
3. Mix pork and its marinade in a mixing bowl.
4. Heat oil in wok, stir fry garlic, mushrooms, and marinated pork for 2 to 3 minutes. Spoon ingredients into a mixing bowl and allow to cool for 5 minutes, then mix in gelatine cubes.
5. Divide and spoon filling onto each 8 pieces of wrapping. Lift up two opposite tips of each wrap and then make a half turn to close the wrap.
6. Line a bamboo steamer basket with a leaf of nappa cabbage. Place dumplings inside steamer and steam under high heat for 6 minutes.
7. Serve hot with dipping sauce.

B-B-Q Pork Bun
With Oyster Sauce

This popular dim sum dish is delicious with green tea. The use of store-bought dough and B-B-Q pork make this dish super easy to make.

Prep Time   15 minutes
Cooking Time   8 minutes

Makes 4

12	oz	Pillsbury Original / Buttermilk Biscuit
1	tbsp	Flour
1	tsp	Corn Oil

Filling

1	tbsp	B-B-Q Pork, diced (or Ground Pork)
½	tsp	Oyster Sauce (or Hoy Hsin Sauce)
½	tbsp	Cornstarch

1. In a small saucepan, combine ingredients for filling. Turn stove on medium-low and heat ingredients for 1 minute. (If ground pork is used, extend cooking time for another half-minute, or until pork is at least 90% cooked). Divide pork mixture into 4 parts.
2. Open the Pillsbury biscuit dough. Cut into 2 parts. Take a part to a lightly floured work surface. Further divide dough into 4 small parts. Press down the centre of each dough with your thumb. Spoon one part of the B-B-Q pork mixture from Step 1 onto the centre of each dough. Wrap up dough and twist close its top.
3. Cut 4 pieces of 2 in. x 2 in. square parchment paper. Grease each piece with some oil and then place under a B-B-Q pork bun. Take out two bamboo steamer baskets and put 2 buns in each.
4. Fill some water in a wok. Cover and then turn stove on medium. When water is simmering, stack up the two bamboo baskets and place them into the centre of wok. Cover the top basket with a lid. Steam until the B-B-Q pork buns are well expanded and dry on the surface, about 8 minutes. Serve at once.

Shrimp CheungFan
Rice Rolls With Soy Sauce

Other than shrimp, either beef, fish, pork liver, fried bread stick or vegetables can be used as fillings. Cheungfan is typically served with oil and soy sauce or chilli sauce.

Prep Time	15 minutes
Cooking Time	8 minutes

Makes 3

3		Vietnamese Rice Paper	Sauce		
1	tsp	Corn Oil or Peanut Oil	1	tbsp	Corn Oil or Peanut Oil, pre-cooked
			1	tbsp	Light Soy Sauce

Filling		
9		Mediium Size Shrimps, shelled and deveined
½	tsp	Sesame Oil
1/8	tsp	Pepper
½	tbsp	Cornstarch
1	tbsp	Spring Onion, chopped, divided into 3 parts

1. In a small mixing bowl, marinate shrimps with sesame oil, pepper and cornstarch.
2. Fill a large bowl with some water, soak a Vietnamese rice paper in the water for 2 seconds. Transfer to a work surface (e.g., a large tray or a cutting board) that has been lightly greased with corn oil.
3. Evenly place 3 shrimps along the centre line of the rice paper. Sprinkle one-third of the chopped spring onions on top. Roll up rice paper and place it on a heat-proof dish.
4. Repeat steps 2 and 3 to make the other two cheungfan rice rolls.
5. Steam cheungfans over medium-high heat for 8 minutes. Serve with oil and soy sauce.

LoBakGo Pudding
Savoury Turnip and Sausage Pudding

This savoury pudding can be enjoyed either steamed or pan-fried. What used to be a festive food for the Chinese New Year has become a favouite year-round dim sum.

Prep Time	20 minutes		
Cooking Time	90 minutes		

Serves 6 - 8

1/4	Turnip (White Raddish), about 2½ cups, peeled and julienned (save juice)	½	cup	Rice Flour
		2	tbsp	Cornstarch
		½	tbsp	Corn Oil or Peanut Oil
1	Pork Sausage, chopped			
1	Bacon, chopped		Marinade	
5	Dried Shrimp, pre-soaked in water for an hour, peeled and chopped	1	tsp	Chicken Powder
		½	tsp	Five Spice
		1/8	tsp	Pepper
1	Shiitake Mushroom, pre-soaked in water for an hour, stem removed and chopped	1	pc	Rock Sugar, about the size of a 25-cent coin

1. Heat oil in a frying pan, under medium heat, stir-fry dried shrimp, shiitake mushroom, sausage and bacon for about 2 minutes.
2. Pour turnip juice (if any) into a measuring cup. Top up with water to the 1-cup mark.
3. In a medium size saucepan, make a dry well with rice flour and cornstarch. Pour liquid from Step 2 into the centre. Use a wooden spoon and stir until mixture is smooth. About 3 minutes.
4. Heat oil into a non-stick frying pan, add turnip and marinade. Stir fry under medium heat until turnip is tender and translucent, about 20 minutes. Add water from time to time to keep turnip from burning. Add ingredients from Step 1 to frying pan. Stir fry for a minute. Turn off heat.
5. Pour ingredients from Step 4 into the saucepan that contains mixture formed in Step 3. Turn heat to low, use a wooden spoon to stir mixture from time to time until thickened. Pour mixture into a 7" cake mould. Steam cook under Medium-High heat for 75 minutes. Serve immediately or continue to Step 6.
6. (Optional) Let LoBakGo pudding cool off and refrigerate overnight. Cut up pudding into 1/4 inch thick rectangular slices. Heat ½ *tsp* oil in a non-stick frying pan, under low heat, pan-fry each side of LoBakGo slices for about 5 - 8 minutes, or until golden brown. Serve hot with or without chilli sauce.

DESSERT

Ma Lai Go

Steamed Sponge Cake

A pound cake cooked on a steamer, the result is a cake that is light and spongy. Ma Lai Go sponge cake is a welcomed alternative to traditional rice buns and rice cakes for many Chinese children.

Prep Time	20 minutes
Cooking Time	30 minutes

Serves 6

1/3	cup	Butter (at room temperature)
1/3	cup	Sugar
1/3	cup	Honey
3		Large Eggs
½	tsp	Vanilla Extract
2	tsp	Baking Powder
1	cup	All Purpose Flour
1/3	cup	Milk (at room temperature)

Lining for Steamer Basket

1	tbsp	Butter
1	pc	Parchment Paper

1. Mix sugar, honey, eggs, butter and vanilla extract together with an electric mixer. Beat until smooth.
2. Add baking powder, flour and milk. Beat until a smooth, thick batter forms. Pour into the prepared steamer basket.
3. Take out the steamer basket insert and fill water into a steamer boiler, turn on high heat and bring water to a boil.
4. Line the steamer basket insert by placing a piece of parchment paper that has been cut out to fit the size of the steamer basket. Grease the parchment paper with butter.
5. Pour batter into steamer basket and steam over high heat for 30 minutes.
6. Remove from steamer. Let stand for 5 minutes to cool. Cut into wedges and serve.

New Year NinGo
Red Dates Curd

The sweet and gooey dates curd is best eaten warm when pan-fried with a thin coating of egg. It is a tradition to enjoy this sweet treat with family and friends during Chinese New Year.

Prep Time   10 minutes
Cooking Time   50 minutes

Serves 4

1/4	cup	Glutinous Rice Flour
½	cup	Water
½	cup	Brown Sugar
½	cup	Dried Red Dates
1	tsp	Corn Oil or Peanut Oil

1. Soak dried red dates in room-temperature water for 2 hours or until soft. Remove peels and pits. Mesh.
2. In a large mixing bowl, mix together glutinous rice flour and brown sugar. Add water and meshed dates. Use a wooden spoon to stir mixture together for about 3 minutes. Pour into a heat-proof bowl that has been greased with corn oil.
3. Steam over medium-high heat for 50 minutes. Cool and refrigerate overnight.
4. Cut NinGo dates curd into 1/4 inch thick retangular slices.
5. Beat an egg in a small mixing bowl. brush egg on NinGo slices.
6. Heat oil in a non-stick frying-pan, under low heat, slowly pan-fry date curd slices, abou 5 minutes, turn over to the other side, heat for another 5 minutes or until soft. Serve immediately.

Thai Mango Sticky Rice
With Coconut Cream Sauce

The creamy white sticky rice and the nutty black sticky rice are pleasantly flavoured by the rich coconut cream and the sweet and juicy Ataulfo mango. No wonder it is a favourite among many Thai food lovers.

Prep Time	10 minutes
Material Stand Time	Overnight or at least for 6 hours
Cooking Time	45 minutes

Serves 2

½	cup	Black Glutinous Rice (a.k.a. Black Sticky Rice or Purple Sticky Rice)
½	cup	White Glutinous Rice (a.k.a. Glutinous Rice, White Sticky Rice)
1		Ataulfo Mango, skinned and sliced
½	cup	Coconut Cream

Marinade (Divide into 2 parts)

3-½	tbsp	Brown Sugar
1	tsp	Corn Oil
¼	tsp	Pandan Leaf Extract (a.k.a. Baythoy Extract); alternatively use 2 pcs. of pandan leaves

Coconut Cream Sauce

½	cup	Coconut Cream
1	tbsp	White Sugar
½	tsp	Corn Starch (Optional)
1/8	tsp	Salt

1. Separately rinse black and white glutinous rice under cold tap water for ½ minute. In separate heat-proof bowls, each add water to just cover glutinous rice. Let stand overnight or for at least 6 hours..
2. Steam glutinous rice over medium high heat for 40 minutes or until they are soft.
3. Blend in one-half of the marinade into the black glutinous rice and the other half into the white glutinous rice. Steam for another 5 minutes. Turn off heat. Cover wok.
4. In a small saucepan, mix ingredients for the coconut cream sauce. Turn stove on medium low. Stir until tiny bubbles start to emerge at the rim of the saucepan.
5. Spoon white glutinous rice, black glutinous rice, and sliced mango onto a plate.
6. Pour coconut cream sauce on top. Serve warm.

Index

B

bamboo steamer 11
bean thread vermicelli 22
beef 40
black bean 32, 34
black bean paste 15
boiler 12
brown rice 60
burner setting 8

C

ceramic pot 12
ChenJiang Dark Vinegar, 16
Chicken 46
  Pot Rice 66
chili 42
chili mustard green 40
chinese cheese 19
chinese pork Sausage 20
ChinKiang Black Vinegar 16
Clam 36
Cleaning 6
Coconut Sticky Rice 76
Cooking Time 8
Cooking Wine 17
Corn Oil 15
Crab 34, 44

D

dark soy sauce 14
Dessert 73–77
  Mango Sticky Rice 76
  Steamed Sponge Cake 74
dim sum 22
dipping sauce 10
donabe 12

dried shiitake mushroom 20
dried shrimp 20
Dumpling 70

E

earth pot 12
Egg 34, 56
Egg Curd 56
Egg Plant 54

F

finishing 9
frozen food 22
fuyu 19

G

gan bei 20
garlic 15
ginger 16, 30, 36
ginger cooking wine 18
glutinous rice 22

H

heat-proof dish 13
Herbs and Seasoning 15
hot Oil glazing 10

I

Introduction 3, 3–5
  Utensils 11

L

lap cheong 20
light Soy Sauce 14
Lobster 24
lotus Leaf 16
Lotus Root 50, 52

M

Ma La Go 74
Mango Sticky Rice 76
marinating 7
Meat
  beef 40
  Pork 42
Meat & Poultry 3–5
minced pork 56
mini sticky rice 22
mustard green 21

N

nappa cabbage 44, 70

O

Oil 15
olive and mustard green paste 15
olive and salty mustard green 68
organic rice 60
Oyster 32
oyster Sauce 14

P

parchment paper 13
Pastes 14
peanut Oil 15
plate-pick 13
Pork 34, 42, 68
  Dumpling 70
  Pot Rice 68
Pot and Wok 12
Pot Rice 66
  Chicken 66
  Pork 68
Poultry
  Chicken 46
prawn paste 14
preserved turnip 21
preserved vegetable 21

R

Red Rice 60
red vinegar 16
Rice 60
   Scented 60
   Semi-Milled 60
Rice and Vermicelli 21
Rice Cooking Wine 18
rice wine 16
Rice Wine Sauce 36

S

Safety 10
salmon 30
salted fish 19
salted plum 21
salted radish 21
salted turnip 20
salty mustard green 40
salty prawn paste 14
salty radish 40
salty soybean cheese 19
salty vegetarian cheese 19
Sauces 14
Sauces and Pastes 14
sausage 20, 46, 50, 66
scallion 15
scented rice 60
Seafood 3, 3–5
   Clam 36
   Crab 34
   Lobster 24
   Oyster 32
   Salmon 30
   Shrimp 28
   Squid 26
sesame oil 15
Shao Hsin rice cooking wine 18
Shiitake Mushroom 46, 66
shiitake mushroom 20

shrimp 28, 52
shrimp paste 14
Siu Lung Bao 70
Siu Lung Bao Dumplings 22
Soup-filled pork fumpling 70
sour plum 21, 42
soy sauce 14
special handling 9
Sponge Cake 74
spring onion 15
Squid 26
stainless steal Steame 11
Steamed Sponge Cake 74
steamer 11
steamer, bamboo 11
Sticky Rice 64
   With Chicken 64
   With Sausage 62
Sticky Rice Wrap 64
sun-dried scallop 20
sun dried scallop 50, 52
sweet potato 54

T

Technique 6
   Cooking 8
   Finishing 9
   Preparation 6
tofu 28

U

Utensils 11
   Heat-proof Dish 13
   Plate-pick 13
   Pot 12
   Steamer 11
   Wok 12

V

Vegetable

Lotus Root 50, 52
Vegetable & Egg 3–5
   Shiitake Mushroom 20
vermicelli 22, 32

W

Wine
   Rice 16
wok 12

Y

yam 54
Yiu Chu 20
Yuem Bai 20
Yun Cheong 20

Z

ZhenJiang Black Vinegar 16

About the author

Fiona Fung is a Chinese Canadian who enjoys cooking and eating healthily. Steam Cooking is her first book.

Acknowledgement

Fiona Fung would like to thank her family for their patience, support and encouragement. Without which, the completion of this book would not be possible.

Special thanks to Chopstick Republic (*www.chopstickrepublic. com*) and EMF Inc. (*www.emf-housewares.com Tel: 416-502-2273*). These companies have graciously lent out many beautiful tablewares, utensils and cookwares for use in this book.

Special Offer

Visit Chopstick Republic (*www. chopstickrepublic.com*)and get $5 off on any purchase totaling $35 or more before tax and shipping.

Simply enter eCoupon code at checkout:
Stzq01pj08

Valid through June 15th, 2009

Printed in the United States
142991LV00002B